Made in the USA
Monee, IL
12 August 2021

75508040R00056